PERIPHERAL VISION

MARY ELISABETH THAYER

XANTHUS PRESS
NEW YORK

Library of Congress Catalog Number: 94-60903

ISBN: 0-9638295-3-X

Cover photograph/Tom Graves
Cover design/Laurie Douglas

Printed in the U.S.A.

Xanthus Press
71 Franklin Street
NY NY 10013

CONTENTS

For my father and mother
whose love fueled my life.

Mary Elisabeth Thayer

PERIPHERAL VISION

THE POPLAR TREE

My brother planted that poplar by the porch.
Father sat, in this same chair,
feet on the railing, hands behind his head,
and over the years, watched with quiet joy
the growth of tree and boy.

This brother could make music out of anything—
even his hands could sing.
Owls hooted through his cupped fingers,
or those same fingers quick and facile
could notch a willow stick
and make a whistle.

He could outwhistle birds,
and finally words were his music,
for, as Father taught, so he grew up to teach,
and made a kind of music out of speech.
No tongue for long was foreign to his tongue;
strange rhythms flowed from his easy voice,
as easy as those owl calls long ago.

Now only the tulip tree and I are left
to wait for the late stars.
They blossom above the hill.
Now and then one falls.
A real owl calls.
In the tree a light wind moves
and all that lost music gathers in its leaves.

LETTING GO

Darling, do you remember
the October morning we stood
by the bedroom window
bewitched by the gingko tree?
Each leaf was a perfect fan,
each fan pure gold.
No breath of wind began it,
but slowly by twos and threes
the leaves began to fall,
slowly steadily falling
until in an hour the show was over.
The little tree stood naked,
stretching her spindly arms
with her petticoat round her feet.

JET

Look at the sky: some fabulous snail
has left a track, dissolving, pale,
yet curiously direct, exact,
not at all what you'd expect.
(Snails meander,
criss-cross wander
back and forth upon a stone,
purpose and direction gone.
They leave an aimless starry scrawl
on garden walk and wall.)
This one on some blue errand bent
unerring went, aslant
across the April heaven,
leaving this incongruous, even
signature upon the sky.
It disturbs the lazy eye.
Accustomed to the shimmering, hazy
April air, we stare uneasy —
can we invent
some code to find out what is meant?
Perplexed, we watch it where
it disappears upon the air.
We cannot read the tall
handwriting on this enormous wall.

THE VIEW

The hills beyond the river drew me in.
They seemed, from where we stood, entirely blue,
but in a longing rush, I knew
the filtered gold, the thronging green
of fern and laurel, all the apparel
of the woods my childhood learned to know
green Aprils long ago.

"Look," I said. "Look at the hills."
"Look at the plain," you said.
"The level land between us and the river
is flat terrain; a good position to defend,
here by this bend of river with the hills behind.
Put mortars there along that ridge beyond the bridge
and twenty men could hold this hill."

What diverse paths we find,
trapped in the heart, mapped in the mind.
Look two ways at a blue hill
and see, in our disparity,
at once our love,
and what it cannot give or prove.
How can this flesh, despite our loving wish
be one, who yet remain irrevocably twain?

PAMELA

For two years she has struggled with the cello.
Envisioning the crowded concert halls,
we set her on the path she was to follow;
for birthday presents, records by Casals.

Sedate at ten, determined to conform,
she yet remains serenely undeterred
at this ungainly venture from the norm;
she mounts her awkward steed without a word.

She bites her lip in eager concentration,
frowns at our foolish impulse to applaud,
and dignity in every unskilled motion,
achieves her private Perpignans and Prades.

Still undismayed, she and her Rosinante
strive cheerfully to attain a mutual grace.
Our hearts transpose her dissonant andante.
There is enough of music in her face.

MAN PLOWING

What does he think about, whose work is solitary,
walking behind the anachronistic horse?
Miles from the highway, up a narrow road,
this rocky slope is his, and the house
and a few acres by the creek.
A pair of jets disturb the tranquil sky,
but if he hears their dim unseasonable thunder
it is not his concern; he will not look up.
Does he see in his mind the young corn growing?
Does he see by the porch the catalpa tree in bloom?
What does he hold in his heart for the woman
who stands on the porch, one hand shading her eyes
against the noon sun? Does he love her?
Do they quarrel? What do they share?
It is all so quiet; even the pale child on the steps
is silent, holding a yellow cat in her arms.
The farm is suspended, hung on this hill
out of time and space, like a place in a dream.
The child sits on the steps,
the woman goes back in the house.
The yellow cat stretches in the sunshine.
Unhurried, the man and the old horse continue
to impose tomorrow's shape upon today.
On the stubborn soil a pattern begins to appear.
Overhead the vapor trails fade slowly on the air.

A QUESTION OF GRACE

Tree leans to greening tree
in the river's quiet surface.
I lean above them both
and ponder grace,

thinking it less a state
than a new dimension,
being to faith perhaps
as love to passion.

As fluid as the air
or the flowing river,
easing for us the stiff
necessities of never.

As April will renew
the fires we thought diminished,
while we unlearn the winter's
long lesson of anguish.

A fine rain falls now
on these distractions.
I share with the swelling river
my green reflections.

IN THE LOOKING GLASS

My mother's hand mirror is heavy silver.
It is richly bordered
with flowers, possibly asters,
in high relief, entwined
with a vine which forms the handle.

On the lower right, in full profile,
is the head of a lovely woman.
Her hair is swept high
on top and caught
at the back by a ribbon.

In the center is an elaborate
initial, P, for Patty,
underneath which
some childish hand, perhaps
my own, has scratched a wavering copy.

All of my childhood I thought
that silver lady
was my pretty mother,
her very own self.
Even now the perfect nose,
the delicate throat,
look like her early pictures—
the picture of her with
my young father,
preparing to sail on the Shinyo Maru
for Yokohama, en route
to Korea as missionaries
nearly eighty years ago.

Did she take her mirror with her?
The rim is dented and scarred.

How brave she was
and how sweet.

My throat is tight with longing
as I turn the mirror over
and search the glass
for the least trace
of her darling face.

JIMMY MAKES IT SNOW

It is one of the hangover picnics.
Often in summer, after a disastrous night,
Rita and Jimmy, Phil and I, collect
our ten children, some eager, others reluctant,
pack an enormous lunch
and set off upriver in Jimmy's boat.

We tie up at a little island.
The kids dive into the water,
shouting and drowning each other,
while we build a fire for the hotdogs.
Then we sit in the sun, dispensing
largesse to our beautiful children.

In November the boat is out of the water,
but we need to salvage the day,
so in two crowded cars
we head for the Blue Ridge Parkway.
Turning off at Rocky Row Run,
we hike maybe half a mile

up the chilly trail, lugging the food,
dragging the littlest children.
They begin to complain, they wrangle and whine.
Jimmy stops. He assumes his God–The–Father voice.
You Children, he says, Be Quiet.
I Am Going To Make It Snow.

We wait in scornful silence.
Then a few flakes fall. Soon
it is snowing quite hard.
The kids go wild, jumping
up and down, sticking out their
tongues to catch snowflakes.

Three of the startled grownups stare
at the fourth. He shrugs.
It's all in Who you know.
And we follow the ecstatic children
down the darkening mountain
through the first lovely snow of the year.

THIS IS HOW IT IS

and sure to get worse
before you know it.
Long-orphaned, now
widowed, the nice
children hundreds
of miles away,
many friends faithless,
a lover unlikely,
my bones complaining,
my fabulous
energies waning.

Then why do I
wake every day of
my life, still crazy
in love with
the whole beautiful world?

RIVER CIRCLE

There was the big pecan tree first
and then, incredibly, the house,
around the final bend in the dusty road,
the country stillness holding it secure,
the wind lifting the leaves in the old trees.
It is still the same,
the musty smell, the cool quiet of the rooms.
The sheep in their gilt frame
still graze serenely over the mantelpiece,
and grandmother in white tulle
peers imperturbably from her wall
at Lee and His Generals opposite.

The barn is the same, dim and fragrant,
the worn roof starred with August sunlight.
The clump of fennel smells of licorice still
and the road is full of walnuts.

Where are the children, laughing in the river?
Where are the horses
and the foals with children's names?
Where are the dogs who sang on the hill at night?
(You knew them by their voices: Corbin, Shady, Rex.)

It is a long time since we sat on the twilit steps
and watched the shadows gather across the field.
The roads we travel now are divided highways.
None of them lead to the farm.
Miles apart, we nurse our separate griefs,
little by cherished little relinquishing the fire,
uneasy, unable, adjusting effect to cause,
fraying toward age.

If there is peace at all
it is in a place, not in the heart.
It hangs here over the boxwood and the beech tree,
and sits by the fireplace where we talked til dawn.

O come to the farm again, come back
while there is time, to the circling river,
and the old house and the sweet smelling barn.

RAKING LEAVES

Now the spring and summer
lie gathered at my feet.
The April stammer
in my blood is this neat

pile of leaves. The smoke
curls from the lighted match.
I lean on the rake
as the flames rise, and watch.

Now it is time to wait
for a different weather,
time for the separate
to draw together.

Now it is time to turn
inside, and close the door,
where the slow-banked fires burn,
and the blood speaks slower.

FATHER'S FIREWORKS

This is a far cry
from the Fourth of July when I was little.
Then small boys
with pockets full of noise
banged their way
through the loud and lovely day.
Flags flew.
Father put ours out
before we had breakfast,
but we knew,
oh, even when we were small we knew
that if the exploding day was our delight,
his was the night.
The air about his pulpit had been bright
for years with pinwheels and salutes.
His thought gathered and burst and blossomed
like giant Roman Candles.
No music of Handel's ever was as full
of fireworks as Father was on Sunday.
Here then was one day that surely
suited him entirely.

As soon as it was dark we went in cars
to a hill he knew
and began to make stars.
Oh it was magic, the sky was a garden,
crimson, purple, green —
We said each year was the best we had ever seen.
We were hopelessly greedy.
We said "Is it over already?"
and wailed as we watched
the last silver shower fall,
and sadly got back in the cars,
Father saddest of all.

Well, we will go on a picnic and take the children,
with red, white and blue paper plates
and maybe some sparklers.

They will be pleased with these and wave them wildly
in the gathering dark
until at last the only spark
is the fireflies' intermittent amber,
and we will be still, and watch, and remember.

EDITH, ON THE PORCH

Propping her elbow on the chair's arm,
she leans into the late September sun;
one hand shading her eyes against the light,
she watches shadows creep across the lawn.

Pale and spent, this sun will never warm
her sweatered bones, as brittle as a bird's.
She does not hear the noisy children calling to one another
in the adjoining yards.

Those other children, none of them her own,
throng the long years muddled in her head.
She ponders them with wonder and mild longing.
They gave her her one treasure: their brief need.

The shadows lengthen in the fading light.
She hitches her chair into the remaining sun,
and props her head once more upon her hand.
Muttering, musing, dozing, she waits her turn.

MACAROONS

January twentieth, my father's birthday.
He was the age I am now
when he died forty years ago. Today
I bake him his favorite cookies.

The froth of the egg white and sugar,
the flowery smell of almond paste,
bring me a noseful of memories,
like the acrid smell of the sassafras tea

he made from a bundle of little roots
he bought at the city market
and brewed in a thick aluminum cup
I use nearly every day.

The smell of his pipe. Everything
smelled of that pipe, his hands, his hair,
the viyella smoking jacket
I made him the year I took sewing lessons.

I see him in that jacket at bedtime
carefully banking the fire with ashes.
In the morning he would poke out
a live coal to light his pipe.

I remember the new car smell of the big Packard
he loved to polish with a silk handkerchief,
and the armful of lilac he brought
to the hospital when my first daughter was born.

I had not seen him in months when one night
I sat up in bed stark awake.
"Sir?" I answered aloud, "Yes Sir?"
Unlike young Samuel in the temple I knew who called me.

Next morning my mother phoned to say
father died in his sleep last night.
I still wonder what he wanted to tell me
as I sit here eating his macaroons.

A LEVEL VIEW

Far up the beach
figures on tiny legs
run busily back and forth
at the water's edge.

The fishing pier beyond
is a frail extent
of match-stick pilings. A bridge
in a Japanese print.

Lying flat and sill
in the hot sand,
I watch the dune grass lean
heavily in the wind,

until I turn my head
at last, for a change of view,
and suddenly all I see
in this long world is you,

leaning there above me,
smiling for no reason.
I realize once more —
you are my horizon.

THE POND AT CADY'S MILL

Waiting for thrush time I sit
on the dock of the pond and do
what I spend half my life doing:
I look at trees and water.

On the bank to the east are dark pines
and oaks, their new foliage a cloud
of foggy grey against green
of sweet gum and tulip poplar.

I remember how at Ravenna
the pictures of the mosaics
seemed somehow more dazzling
than the mosaics themselves.

Here the mirrored trees,
the mosaic of leaf and bark
full length in the still water
are beautiful almost beyond bearing.

I walk through the beech grove down
to the creek. Beside the path
an old black metal chair
has been slip-covered by a wild rose.

Back at the dock the thrushes
are tuning their flutes. A breeze
has come up and the perfect trees
are drowned in the trembling water.

FOR ADIN

You were eighteen that summer when the swan
swam out of darkness on the midnight lake,
while dreaming there below us stood Chillon,
casting a spell too magical to break.
Intact, entire, preserved like bees in amber,
the night was added to your store of grace.
In less auspicious years I will remember
the wonder written on your quiet face.
Now over waters wider than Lac Leman,
you on the longest journey soon must start.
The perilous business of becoming woman
has need of treasures hidden in the heart.
Then cherish joy, most private, precious daughter—
hold fast the swan upon the trembling water.

AFTER SOME YEARS

What has changed? Can you tell?
We who knew well
the warm climate of our mutual seasons,
now for separate reasons
endure a different weather,
wary of one another,
who find we share
warmth without fire.
We peer past thresholds still uncrossed,
wondering what was lost.
Oh, nothing is lost that was ours to lose
who could blend but never fuse.

QUANDARY

In the spring after my father died
I took Mother for a long ride.
We drove a country road between
fields newly green.
Hands folded in her lap, tranquil, still,
she rode in easy silence, till—
Now how will I ever know, I heard her say,
which in the world is oats and which is hay?

THE WILLOW PRINCESS

Spring begins in the trees.
In my mind it begins
in the willow tree in the side yard
in my green childhood.
The sycamores still were ghosts,
the pink fire of the maple weeks away
when suddenly one day
outside my window the willow
was calling, calling, calling.

I braided its long branches
into intricate passageways,
room after waving room,
a palace for a princess.
In my book of fairy tales
there was a tree like this,
dripping jewels, emeralds and rubies
into the hands of a lady with long fingers,
and a long dress, and long golden hair.
There was no prince in the picture.

And still year after spinning year
the greening willow beckons,
summoning me
to the lost contentment
of the lonely princess
in the willow palace.

REPORT FROM THE ISLAND
October

There on the rocks where in summer
you clean your daily catch,
and the gulls come for the leavings,
the fish heads and their delicate entrails,
I have thrown
some scraps from the fridge,
a few muffins, half a loaf of my own bread.

At once,
off the sun-dazzled water,
out of the immaculate sky,
a constellation of birds has appeared
to celebrate the mass,
shattering the shining air with their raucous
Kyrie! Kyrie! Kyrie!

Soon they disperse
and I am left with the wine,
a little Chablis,
which, blessed, I will drink
to the glory of God and His creatures,
not excluding, oh Lord, your humbled servant,
myself.

When I fall on my knees
with my face to the rising sun,
oh Lord, have mercy on me.

MOURNING LELLIE

The shock of your death, even now
a year later, wakes me sometimes
in the night, longing to say
goodby – or hello. I couldn't
imagine how much I would miss you,
you with your caustic wit,
your clever hands, your pretty legs.

The last child in the family,
nearly five years after you,
I nudged you off the primordial throne,
our mother's lap. If you begrudged me
that spot, you never showed it.
We shared houses, clothes, took care
of each other's babies, took care
of each other for most of our long lives.

Three summers ago, watching you sneeze,
I asked if you were allergic.
I'm allergic to life, you answered.
That answer lies like a stone on my heart.
Oh sister, what sadness were you carrying
so bitter that we couldn't share it?

In my kitchen is a little night light
you made of a shell you brought home
from Virgin Gorda. I forget it
by daylight, but often in the loneliest
hour of the night, I find you there waiting
to welcome me to the dark.

FOR LAURIE

Few things solace the heart savaged by pity.
Resolve in the wake of grief wanes;
the grief remains.

But laurel leaning through shadows above the stream,
water falling on stone,
the wood-thrush at dawn,

these comfort. These, and sunlight on water, and
always trees, with the sun sifting through.
And oh darling, you.

NOW IS NOT INSTEAD

Now is the music in my blood,
now is the golden tree
starred with a dazzled beauty
like the starred and dazzled sea.
Now is not instead.

Now is the taste of sorrow
mingled sweet and sour
like apples in the autumn.
Now is the infinite hour.
Now is not tomorrow.

Now is the flame and the fire,
now is the running child,
now is the hidden flower,
the hidden bird in the field.
Now is my love entire.

Now is the gift that is given,
now giver and gift are one.
The bright rain on the leaf
shines in the sudden sun,
and now is my sudden heaven.

OCTOBER 22   3:18 P.M.

The moment is hung between breath and breath,
not death in life, not life in death,
nothing begun nor ended,
but time suspended —
the wind stilled,
the cold light held
in a perfect slant across this single tree.
Caught in the crystal quiet, free
from the pull of wish and will
this now is all.
I lie here
returning the day's blue stare.
One leaf falls for a token
The bright spell is broken.

IDENTITY

Water on stone
and the branches leaning above.
This stream is all
in the world I love.

No thing in life,
no dear face,
was ever as dear to me
as this place.

Far on up the mountain
in a green wood,
the source rises
in solitude,

rises out of the earth,
and begins to shape
its singular difficult bed
down this slope.

And I have always known
what it meant
to fall on stone
in a sharp descent,

and follow a stubborn course
down a hill,
and come at last
to a still pool.

The laurel tenderly leans
above the stream.
Oh this is all I love,
and all I am.

PHIL PRAYS FOR JIMMY

Upstairs in surgery
Jimmy is under the knife.
Downstairs we sit long hours
in the waiting room.
When Rita says: Someone should pray,
Phil's good hand shoots up
like a child in school.
Me, he says.

But Phil, with his beautiful voice,
his flawless inflections,
who played Willy Loman and Henry Higgins,
who read aloud Yeats and Auden and Lorca,
Phil has lost all of his words.
Stroke has left him nearly speechless.

No matter. His anguish is for his friend.
He remembers cold Saturdays hunting
to the clamorous music of dogs.
He remembers the long nights boozing
and the bitter wrath of wives.
He remembers the river picnics with all of the kids,
the raucous all night cast parties after plays.

He begins his prayer.
Love is the language,
for the words are not real words,
but we hear the unfolding of wings
as his blessing fills the air.

NO EXIT

We had hung a light high up in the big magnolia
and raked up the leathery leaves below.
It made a dim enchanted playhouse
as we sat there one night with our wine,
Phil and I, Margaret and Rita.

Suddenly something flew into my ear.
Irritating at first, it was quickly unbearable.
The frantic flailing, the magnified buzzing noise
in that unimaginable tunnel
drove me wild.
It couldn't get in, it couldn't get out
and it couldn't die.

Rita took me to the Emergency Room where a doctor
extracted with tiny tweezers a battered moth
an inch long, finally dead.

Awake sometimes in the night I am that moth
bruising my wings against the darkness.

THE SLEEPING PORCH

Two blankets, clothespinned
to a wire, divided in half
the cots on the long porch,
girls on one side, boys on the other.
What did they fear,
the long-ago parents who
hung up those blankets?
We were too many for mischief,
a covey of cousins, six or eight
little kids, six or eight years old.
Bedded down for the night,
admonished to silence,
the least thing would set us off.
The smallest deliberate fart
provoked such howls of laughter
that threats came up through the floor
from the grown-ups who
rocked on the porch below.
We subsided to whispers,
but sleep had to capture
us one by reluctant one.

The cots sagged in the middle,
the wind blew rain
through the screen, in a
hard rain the roof leaked,
while all in a row
like dolls in a cupboard,
we slept cocooned, and wrapped
in more love than we
ever would know again.

THIS CHILD

She cannot whisper, cannot walk;
such urgency informs her talk
that she must evidence her need
at full voice and at full speed.
What burden of necessity
provides and guides this energy?
Merry, willful, quick and proud,
often bloody, seldom bowed,
she pursues her errant way
stubbornly through every day.
Helpless with astonishment,
I feel the force of her intent
and wonder how she came to see
with such singularity.
Her means may obviate their ends;
she will break before she bends.
Oh, but if she learns to love
she will make the mountains move!

MOTHER'S DYING

Last year I read of a vicious creature, the giant
waterbug. Swimming beneath a frog, for example,
sunning himself half-on, half-off a rock
in a creek, the waterbug (in fact, an enormous beetle)
seizes his legs, and injects an enzyme so lethal
that the frog, all but his glistening skin, is dissolved,
reduced to a juice. A cup of instant frog
for the greedy shadow beneath the shining water.

Last month I sat all night by my mother's bed,
now and then putting my face against hers, saying,
in hope of some possible contact, first her name,
then my own, but mostly holding her hand,
all night holding her, trying to help her die.
I remembered those books about death and dying,
and longed to see some light on her still face,
not for me, not to acknowledge my presence,
but as if, as she knew she would, she had come to a known
shelter—she whose love had sheltered so many.
What I saw instead was the unseen. Swimming beneath
her bed, the giant waterbug, death, sipped
my mother away. She diminished hourly. At dawn
her flesh lay on her beautiful bones like the Chinese
silk she used for her dining room curtains. Her skin
was pongee. Toward noon, the barely perceptible breathing
stopped, but so gently that leaning to kiss her cheek
I found she had gone without my even knowing.

THE SHOWY ORCHIS

Deep in the wood where no one ever came,
there was the flower where you said it was;
too small entirely for its showy name,
Orchis Spectabilis. Still, that day, because
we had found it there in that disorder
of rock and leaf and fern, seen it and known it,
we dug it up and took it for our border,
moved by some dear necessity to own it.
As if discovery did not impart
its own possession; already it was ours
who claimed it for the climate of the heart.
Often, in deeper woods then these, love flowers,
in poorer soil and less auspicious weather.
Having and holding are different altogether.

A LESSON FROM RODIN

"Never overlook the slightest thing which can give rise to joy."
                                    —Auguste Rodin quoted by Rilke

Joy comes in at the
eye and goes straight
to the brain
which sends arpeggios coursing
along the veins.

For an instant the
shutter opens and look!
Tiepolo's clouds are above
your house, the white
heron lights on the
treetop, the kingfisher
dives for his dinner,
the child throws back her
head in an ecstasy of laughter,
and along the street, in
perfect sync, a red-headed
girl jogs with her
Irish setter, his hair the
same color as hers.

Look again. Fold
on blue fold the mountains
cradle the valley
where the young peach
orchard blooms. Sun's
alchemy sifting through
trees pans gold in
the rocky creek. Just
before sunrise five swans
fly over the cove. A
fingerling moon, a
silver minnow, swims
in the August sky.

Joy perceived is a habit of
being. Believing is seeing.

GOLDFINCHES

Suddenly all that blue
air broke into bright
scallops of delight—
goldfinches flew!

Their even grace,
perfect as Mozart,
quickened the heart
as a loved face

will shorten its beat.
Then they were gone.
Always too soon,
What is most sweet

will fill the air
and dazzle the sight
like birds in flight—
then disappear.

KOMM SÜSSER TOD

Crippled by stroke, virtually speechless,
he decided four years was enough.
Trapped in his alien body,
his mind, still his own,
found an acceptable out.
He refused all the medications
calibrated to keep him alive,
to ward off heart failure,
blood clots, massive arrhythmia.
Then with the doctor's consent
and morphine as needed
we began our mortal vigil.

He never wavered.
He laughed with the children,
and chose for each one a gift,
his gold watch, his Silver Star,
for earlier gallantry in action,
the print of the book stalls beside the Seine,
his Lautrec etching,
his bronze Napoleon.

The afternoon of the third day
he swung his legs over
and sat on the side of the bed
looking into the mirror,
a long, long look,
telling himself goodby.
Then he looked at me.
You and me, pointing to each,
then a circle
with thumb and forefinger — "Good," he said.
I put my arms around him,
holding him close,
and at that moment
without any warning,
he drew three great shuddering breaths,
his body sagged against mine
and then praise God
he was gone.

ECCLESIASTES AT LUNCH

A woman sat at my table
holding a sick child in her arms.
The rest of us argued God's rumored demise,
and duty, parental and otherwise.

She said, in a lull,
"Well—all I know about life is:
revere it."

GRIEF

When it was over
I thought you would lurk in ambush
to take me by surprise.
How wrong I was.
You share my house, my wine, my bed.
You are my familiar.

Come with me now to the market
to buy turnips and fresh peas.
Sit with me on my comfortable sofa
and listen to "Death and the Maiden."
Walk with me down to the river
to wait by the tracks
and watch the long train
go empty back to the coal fields.

Then come with me to the kitchen
while I wash lettuce
and shell the peas for my supper,
and after I read the evening away,
at bedtime, lay your head on my pillow.

ESCAPE ARTIST

"For there the snake throws her enamelled skin,
weed wide enough to wrap a fairy in."
                              —Shakespeare
                    "A Midsummer Night's Dream"

Blacksnake, slitherer,
when did you pour yourself
into my attic, through
a door so tiny
even the rain couldn't enter?
Flowing into the dark, you lay
coiled, waiting for mice.
Below you, curled
in my nest of down,
I lay waiting for sleep.

This morning, climbing
those treacherous pull-down steps
to put away winter clothes,
I found you
had put yours away already.
I wish I had been there.
I would love
to watch you disrobe, you
who could teach Houdini
a lesson.

PICTURES ON THE FRIDGE

The hosts of the Lord have
encamped in my kitchen.
Look at their darling faces!
Oh children of my children,
emissaries from on high,
I will sing you the litany.

Oh, all ye whales and fishes and Molly and Alden,
praise ye the Lord!
Oh all ye beasts of the field and Jessica and Luke,
praise ye the Lord!
Oh all ye birds of the air and Lucy and Nora and Anna,
praise Him and magnify Him forever!

And Philip, my handsome husband,
not considered a saint
in your time on earth,
still I say to you:
by just so much light
as has gone from my life
are the halls of heaven brightened.

So I praise professors and cooks,
for I think at this very moment,
having dismissed the angels
from their class on the French Revolution,
you are teaching the Most High
how to make
watercress soup.

THINKING OF FRANCES

So here I am by my fire this winter night,
bitter for us. Seven inches of unsouthern snow
blanket the mountains that lie between our houses,
but tonight you are nearer, wired as if for some
monstrous experiment in a room called Intensive Care.
They will monitor you, and read all the hieroglyphics
the clever needles inscribe, but my dear, no machine
knows as well as you the intricacies of nurture.
That tightrope-walker, your husband, needing you always
for ballast, his mother, your father, five children, grandchildren,
foals, calves, and the young fruit trees to save
from the killing frost. It was all intensive care.
I think of you with such love, but I think of your face
with awe. When Yeats speaks of Maud Gonne's 'eagle look'
I see your face with the mountains in your eyes.
In a few days they will let me come to your room,
and instead of flowers, I will bring you this for a mirror.

SCENE AT THE TABLE

There is a pattern in the cloth,
flowers and squares. A small moth,
blinded, likely, by the light
went round and round in a white
square, seemingly unable
to free himself from this bright table.
I too have often been
in his dilemma; time and again
prevented by the shape of things
from lifting wings.

DRY SPELL

1

Three months ago I walked this wood
to look for lady's slippers.
Now as the summer tapers
to its grudging end, the road
is dry. Even the lizards tire
of August; startled, they flash
into the dusty brush
beside the track, where
Indian pinks were thick in May.
In the grey shade, ferns
wither; a dove mourns.
Now nothing green can grow,
and I, caught in a dry spell,
walk in a daze,
hearing the jarflies buzz,
hearing the dove call,
remembering all I had
in April. The anemones are gone,
April is years ago. In the hot sun
by the dry road, I gather goldenrod.

2

All morning a dove cried
from the woods beside
the window. The low call
hung and fell,
grieving the heavy air,
too sad to bear.
Then toward noon
the long rain began,
easy and warm,
more like a dream
of rain, as sweet and slow
as the mourning cry
of the bird.

In the garden the hard
earth drank. Then the rain
stopped, and soon
the dove began again to plead,
voicing some need,
perhaps her own,
and surely mine—
both sad without reason
in a slack season.

PERIPHERAL VISION

Against a fence
out of the intense heat
of the noon sun,
eight black and white cows
lie with their young
in the deep shade
of a giant oak.
Glimpsed in passing,
serene as Constable,
a family of shadows,
they rest in my speeding brain.

SPRING COMING THIS YEAR WITHOUT MOTHER

"...winter is come and gone,
but grief returns with the revolving year."

—Shelley

Oh it is all beginning again,
the willows greening,
the shadblow hung in the woods
like a handful of stars,
the weeping cherry dipping
pale fingers into the pool
still clogged with the winter's leaves.
The dogwood is in its Chinese phase,
each partially opened blossom a pure celadon,
and beside the stream the fiddleheads
are orchestrating the spring.

I quicken with the season,
unfolding with each leaf,
but waken daily to an unremembered anguish.
Sleep leaves a tabula rasa.
The morning writes her name.

If she is nowhere
how can the bloodroot star the garden
and the oriole nest in the orchard?

Grief returns with each revolving day.
How could I know when we buried her in November
that spring would be altered forever?

FOR META IN HER EIGHTH MONTH

Last of my five, I watch you
awaiting your second.
Abstracted, you sit
with your hands on top
of the globe of the world
in your lap.

Who sleeps in that watery world?
Tethered to you
in that warm room
does your baby dream?

In another watery world
your four year old sings.
So precious is she, this first born,
that you fear your heart cannot hold
more love than you have for her.

But think of your grandmother.
You, fifteenth
of her sixteen grandchildren—
could she have loved you more?

Think of your sisters before you.
You are on love's continuum.
Full measure, pressed down,
shaken together, running over,
there will be love enough
and to spare.

TAKING THE WATERS

The pontifical baby,
two weeks old, lies
in the tub on a
clever sponge, shaped
like the bottom half
of a mold for
making babies.

At the rim of
his world, sister,
grandmother, father
and mother kneel
in a rapt silence
as if they expect
him to speak. Instead
his sea anemone fingers
open and close,
open and close,
open and close.

THE ART OF SELF-DEFENSE

She is walking up Fifth Street, the middle
of Fifth Street, in heavy traffic,
a gray haired woman thin as a knife,
pushing a grocery cart spilling over
with clothes, shoes, dishes, a ruffled
pink satin pillow, and pulling along
on a rope a scruffy white dog.
I turn the corner and double park,
leaving the two grandchildren,
Luke and Jessy, aged eight and ten.

Cars swerving around us,
I ask if she wants a ride.
She follows in a sullen silence,
and watches me wrestle her cart
into the tailgate. I open
the right front door. She slams it shut
and crowds in back with the children,
dragging the dog up into her lap.

Her destination is not
a few blocks, but ten miles or more
across town, down 29 South.
As I drive, I watch
in the rearview mirror
the children's terrified faces.

She never speaks after giving me
her directions. Nobody speaks.
At last we leave her beside
the highway, not a house in sight.
As we start home I ask
"Why were you so frightened, why
was that pool little lady so scary?"
"*Nonna,*" says Jessy,
"all the way out there
that poor little lady
held a huge carving knife in her hand!"

WATER BED

Once we went out
in that ramshackle rowboat
with its fickle outboard,
for a ride, a little
post–prandial ride by starlight.

No stars. Within minutes
we were fog–bound,
all around us an impenetrable scrim.
Ram Island was gone,
the lighted church steeple at Noank,
the nearby lights of our
own house on the point.

So let us, I said,
celebrate this fog,
and our long loving
for we were both past fifty,
and lie down together
in the rocking bed
of the ramshackle rowboat.

CUL DE SAC
The Russian Teacher

Outside the classroom the obscuring snow
is altering again an alien landscape,
where crowding dimly from the encroaching past,
children long dead slide down the shrouded hill,
calling to one another, and to him.

Row on respectful row before him wait
these other children. Eager and inexact,
their tongues will never shape his intricate speech.
Year after year, patient, gentle and tragic,
he labors to instill a strange syntax,
conjugating for them his green childhood,
quietly bridging, phrase after careful phrase,
the treacherous ocean of the past imperfect.

The moment spins. The children's snowy voices
suddenly betray his longing ear,
while under the snow the unfamiliar flowers
cluster again toward April's agony.

VIEW FROM ONION MOUNTAIN
January

No view at all, really. A small ravine
skimpy with laurel, and strewn
with dead chestnut, is all; on the west
I suppose the view is best;
the mountain slopes to a gap, and beyond
of course, lies the promised land,
the gentle valley. Serene, secure
it is faith fulfilled in miniature.
But shivering unfulfilled on a shelf
of lichened rock, I view myself,
of all promised lands least known.
Oh, what red seas lie between
the thickets of will and reason
and the light on the bright horizon?

A MANY-CHAMBERED BOX

Inquisitive John Muir set out
for a walk. "I wish," he said
"I could be more moderate
in my desires, but I cannot,
and so there is no rest."
With that, he left Indianapolis
and walked a thousand
miles to the Gulf of Mexico.

It was an Eden of new
plants and trees. In Georgia
he saw for the first time
a pomegranate. "The fruit,"
his journal notes, "is the
size of an orange, has a
tough thick skin which
when opened, resembles a
many-chambered box full
of translucent purple candies."

Persephone ate some of those
candies, a gift from her
kidnapper-husband. Having
eaten his food, she
must live six months of
each year in his flowerless
underworld. She longs for
Demeter, her grieving mother.
Coming at last together
they invent spring. The whole earth
draws a warm breath. The green begins.
Wherever they walk, lilies
and violets blossom, fruit trees
bloom, the willow, the beech
and the oak unfold their myriad leaves.

And John Muir, taking
his journal, walks in
the deep forest, stepping
carefully, studying mosses,
naming the ferns and the flowers.

ESCAPE

I came here angry to this August hill,
angry that wish and will
refuse to coincide.
I came here to hide.

Deep in the flowered grass
I watch an hour pass.
I watch a hawk wheel in the sky.
A velvet butterfly
wavers upon an orange weed.
I watch my need
diminish as the old loves kindle,
and feel my anger dwindle
until it dies
before my dazzled eyes.

Now in a noon daze,
hugging my mended ways,
I lie at peace in a place
of light and Queen Anne's Lace.

THIS LAST ONE

This one is equable and serene,
no taller than the flowers she walks between
along the path. The Queen Anne's Lace
and goldenrod are level with her face,
and she is singing; all day long
she envelops in an endless song
her three years' experience.
She stops now by the corner of the fence
to look for snails, and finds instead
an early fallen oak leaf, curled and red.
She will bring it in her hand,
and serious, lest I misunderstand,
"This is an angel," she will say.
Leaves are angels. Suddenly my day
is transformed briefly by her magic.
Past and future, all the true and tragic
combine and focus. History
stands smiling in the morning sun at me.

Humbled by eternity so near
I hold her like a shell to my heart's ear.

THE ROAD TO THE ISLAND

for Carol

It is always a tryst with a lover. Every bend
in this road, every stone and tree makes love to me.
The affair will never be over.

And I never will cross this bridge, beloved friend,
without thinking of you. The gulls in their constant reconnaissance
have accepted me in your stead,

but my own heart is less certain. Your singular spirit
inhabits the island, and yearly returning, I find you
palpably here, oh most dear.

Blessed, if not meek, I look at this earth I inherit:
bayberry, shad blow, and the wild cherry bent to the wind
like the trees in your Chinese porcelains.

Patterned with lichen, the enormous rocks still guard
the beds of lemon lilies you loved, as bright
as your irretrievable laughter.

I remember you said once, smiling perhaps at the word,
austere for the girl I was then: "You will be chatelaine
of the island when I am gone."

And I am—or attempt to be. But I daily do homage
to all that precision, all that imperious grace
that you brought, or brought you, to this house.

The skill of your living and dying infects me with courage.
Grateful, I live in your gift, and you in mine
while the sun writes your name on the water.

TOUR JÉTÈ

Driving home alone
on a winter day
thinking mostly of death,
I saw in a bare field
a white dog leap
straight up in the air,
make a half-turn
and land neatly
facing the opposite way.
Precisely as I was passing
he made his leap for me.
Just for me he did his dance.

MISSING PHIL

Oh, the nights I slammed out of the house
sobbing, to walk off my rage
after a fight, careful
not to come home till you were asleep.
Next morning, mean as a snake,
I was mute, immured in the well-known silence,
(who will speak first?)
while the wary children
went willingly off to school.
What a waste, all that energy fueling anger.
How I grieve for that anger now,
longing to hear you come striding home,
your arms full of books and bundles,
calling out Darling! Come look at these lovely
lamb chops!

Only son of a doting mother,
brought up like a crown prince,
why weren't you rotten spoiled?
You wore domesticity
like your bow tie, your blue blazer.
No task was too menial for you.
Today your daughters engage in combat
to compel their men to do
what you did without being asked,
take out garbage, fold laundry,
put kids to bed with stories and songs
(Out in Arizona where the bad men are,
Ragtime Cowboy Joe.)
And the nights you would go in the cold dark
to a sopping squalling baby,
and bring her back dry and powdery
to tuck in the bed between us,
a fledgling in a nest.

What a bore I am at a party.
I have no small talk. Inanities
stick in my throat. Silence ensues.
An uphill hike on a wet trail
is easier than a long dinner.
While you, my dear, when sober,
would scoop up the whole group
in the funnel of your tornado,
everyone laughing and talking, the room
suddenly Oz, and you the wizard.
Weary at length of these takeover tactics
I learned to harden my heart when
the crown prince often turned into a frog
and had to be helped to the car.
Now I sit at my pretty table,
serving my chic little dinner,
thinking why isn't this any fun?
When will this party get started?

WINTER

"One moment of perfect attention is worth a hundred years of kindness."

Zen proverb

Five below. Very cold for Virginia.
From the big kitchen window,
looking down at the river (I am
always looking down at the river)
I see something white in the water.
The binoculars focus on
three tiny ducks,
half the size of a seagull,
black with a white back. Buffleheads.
They look like toys in a tub.
The ponds frozen, they have come
to feed in the river. I watch
their precise choreography.
They swim together, submerge together,
surface together downstream,
repeating their routine over and over.
Pulling a chair to the window,
elbows on the sill to balance the glasses,
I give them my perfect attention.

IN THE WINGS OF THE JUMP

for Edith Jenkins

Today your people
people my mind, For example,
your sister Ethel.
I see you, two little girls
riding the playground donkeys,
you, the littlest,
in a basket seat,
your legs sticking out of the holes
above the donkey's neck.
Years later
you said when she died
you were forced to face
the ultimate loneliness
of the human estate.

I think of your friend, Jean,
and of the note she left—
"To all who loved and helped me,
all love and courage."

And often I think of you
whom I've never met.
Your daughter gave me
your poems four years ago.
It was like a first trip to the Cluny—
infinite riches in a little room.

Awake at 3 A.M.
I took down your book
last night and read it
straight through, for the first time
in over a year.
This morning I learned
you had just had by-pass surgery.
I thought: While I was reading
her poems, she was
in the wings of the jump.
And what emanation
drew me last night to your book?

What can I wish for you, Edith?
Never mind health,
laughter, love, flowers,
sunlight on water.
I wish you
more poems.

SUSPIRATION

I breathe in, a long breath.
Then I breathe out.
In Verona leaves fall from a willow.

I breathe out again.
In Stockholm an old letter blows
down the street.

And you, old friend,
old lover,
no further away than Rhode Island,
is it your breath
I feel on my cheek?

OCTOBER AGAIN

A grey morning, the chill in the air
a blessing after this merciless summer.
An early walk in August
was like swimming through tepid water.

On the lawn four crows caucus. The songbirds,
finch, wren, cardinal, are all silent,
the wood thrush, my heart's music
as rare in Virginia now as a nightingale.

Always at the edge of my comfortable solitude
loneliness waits, desolation waits,
threatening my tenuous truce
between contentment and despair.

VOYEUR

This has been the best year so far,
with a count of fifteen since April,
for Operation Box Turtle.

For years I have stopped by the roadside
to help the box turtle complete
his perilous crossing. Sometimes,
when picked up, he swims his feet
and hisses. Sometimes
he closes his hinged door.

Once I flagged down a large truck.
The driver, annoyed, confused,
slammed on his brakes, crushed the turtle
and came to a stop.
I waved him on.

The bottom shell of the male
is slightly concave, no more
than the palm of your open hand,
but it gives him purchase enough
to rest on her domed back.

This morning I watched from my porch
that precarious mating.
Once settled precisely on top,
he pulled in his legs,
thrust out his long neck
and glared with his red eyes
for six completely immobile minutes.
Then he slipped off
sideways and crawled away.

Small wonder the human life span is so brief.
The turtle may live for a hundred and thirty years.

KISSING

Nothing could stop the squeak of the porch swing
where the heavy chain hung from a hook in the ceiling.
Father one day, despite Mother's protest,
stood on a chair and threaded an unsightly
oiled rag through the offending link.
A few days silence. Then screek, screek.

How many nights did we sit in that swing,
kissing, kissing, our lips firmly closed,
nothing unzipped or unbuttoned,
doing none of the wicked things
we would soon be up to with other people?

It was no sound that got mother
out of her bed upstairs. No screek.
What were we doing down there? (Kissing, kissing)
Adorable creature, everyone loved her,
guarding her three precious daughters
from their nice Presbyterian suitors.
My sisters' beaus called her Old Hawkeye.

In the suspicious silence
she would tip out on the porch above us
and drop a shoe on the floor.
No little curtain lecture, no ultimatum,
just the definitive thunk of the shoe.

HUNGER

The heron sifts down
to the mouth of the cold creek
across the river. For an hour
he stands on one leg
and stares at the pewter water.
He stabs at it once, twice.
Nothing.
At last he furls his long neck
and hunches into the reeds.
Oh heron stay!
I will cross the thin ice of the river
and bring you a platter of eels.

ORION

Living so much alone,
hollowed by grief and loss,
I went for solace
to the dark yard, and stood
looking up at faithful Orion
and the moon through the bare trees.
In that stillness, I was stilled,
all the emptiness suddenly filled,
flooded with an intense awareness
of earth's immense beauty
holding, enfolding me,
touching me everywhere,
compelling a holy gratitude
for all of it, for life, for death,
for my own life
in this moment blessed,
and for Orion
and the moon through the bare trees.

22 OCTOBER IN BEDFORD COUNTY VIRGINIA

Is it time's wingéd chariot at my heel
alerting my senses,
or is the world more beautiful this year?

When I watch at dawn
the silver mist rise from the river
leaving the golden trees in the water,
I quicken, as if
a lover had laid his hand on my breast.

The trees have spread
an intricate Persian carpet on my yard,
fans of gingko, stars of sweet gum,
scarlet of sourwood and maple,
purple and red of dogwood.

And look!
Without a whisper of wind
the hickory is sending down leaves
like a shower of golden coins
in a fairy tale.

Sometimes I have to stop by the highway
to watch the clouds
dreaming their metamorphoses
in the blue October sky.

In the mouth of the creek
across the river
a lone blue heron sojourns.

Riches riches.

Oh when will I ever feel old?

THE ESSENTIAL GIFT

I remember the road from Northampton to Stockbridge, a drive
I took twice a week a few summers ago to see
a doctor at Austin Riggs. I cried and talked,
he listened and now and then made a pronouncement. He said:
in twenty years you have not finished mourning your father.

Well, Father, I think of you now as I sit on the porch
watching the rain come over the mountain.
As a missionary in Korea in 1912,
you must have seen the unwanted baby girls
placed face down on a bed of ashes to die.
Did that memory wait in your heart for your own baby girls?

Your love and energy fueled my life. Armed
with your praise I thought there was nothing I couldn't do.
When I was eight Mother bought me a winter coat.
Take it back, you said to her. Let her choose one herself.
At thirteen you gave me *Crime and Punishment*,
read Browning with me and taught me the constellations.
You took us all up Lookout Mountain to sleep
on a blanket and watch the August meteor shower.
How could a daughter so cherished envy brothers,
and how could *your* daughter be afraid of thunder or snakes?

Solitary yourself, you gave me for an inheritance
the early comfort of my own company:
up in the maple tree by the drive with a book,
hauling my lunch up after me in a basket;
roaming Cherokee Park digging up wildflowers,
rapt on the floor in front of the windup Victrola
listening to Gigli, Caruso, Galli-Curci.
You never said: Go find somebody to play with,
go find a friend. You knew I had found a friend.

Last winter during an ice storm I lived alone
for a week with no heat, no lights, no water, no phone.
It never crossed my mind to desert my house
with branches breaking and trees falling like gunfire
It was you in me, Father, who carried the firewood, hauled
the water, and crunched up the slippery road to survey
the damage, turning disaster into adventure.

73

At peace on the rainy porch, remembering you
in this same split-oak chair with your feet on the railing.
I know the mourning is finished, subsumed in gratitude
for the essential gift, your life in mine.

SWANS

In a lifetime of looking
there's no getting used to swans,
their imperial calm,
their mythic profile in flight.
When they fly low over the house
in the early morning,
my bones melt.

I love their fidelity,
mated for life,
and the family tableau,
dazzling parents
trailing the smoke-colored cygnets.

I love their ferocity,
hissing whenever we come too close,
and their comforting awkwardness
walking onto the rocks,
like me at a large party,
hobbling from topic to topic,
arching my neck to hiss and longing to be,
like swans in water,
back in my natural habitat
solitude.

GRATIAS DEO

The Lenten roses are blooming in the snow.
Gratias Deo.

Mother, nearly ninety,
has finished her breakfast early.
"Now," she says,
"If anyone's going anywhere
I'm ready to go."
Gratias Deo.

The two little spindle-legged goats
come to the fence in the dark dawn
each morning to say hello.
Gratias Deo.

And I live surprised,
feeling tides due to ebb,
instead flow.
Well Gratias. Gratias Deo.